LA SALLE
A LIFE OF BOUNDLESS ADVENTURE

LA SALLE
A LIFE OF BOUNDLESS ADVENTURE

by William Jay Jacobs

Franklin Watts
New York / Chicago / London / Toronto / Sydney
A First Book

Cover illustration by Amy Wasserman
Cover map copyright © North Wind Picture Archives, Alfred, Me.
Cover photograph copyright © New York Public Library, Picture Collection

Photographs copyright ©: New York Public Library, Picture Collection: p. 2;
North Wind Picture Archives: pp. 10, 12, 14, 17, 20, 28, 30, 34, 36, 38, 40, 43, 46, 48,
52, 54; Library of Congress: pp. 23, 32; Stock Montage/Historical Pictures
Service: p. 26; The Bettmann Archive: p. 50.

Library of Congress Cataloging-in-Publication Data

Jacobs, William Jay.
La Salle : a life of boundless adventure / by William Jay Jacobs.
p. cm. — (A First book)
Includes bibliographical references (p.) and index.
ISBN 0-531-20141-4
1. La Salle, Robert Cavelier, sieur de, 1643–1687—Juvenile literature.
2. Explorers—North America—Biography—Juvenile literature.
3. Explorers—France—Biography—Juvenile literature.
4. Mississippi River Valley—Discovery and exploration—French—Juvenile literature.
5. Mississippi River Valley—History—To 1803—Juvenile literature.
6. Canada—History—To 1763 (New France)—Juvenile literature.
[1. La Salle, Robert Cavelier, sieur de, 1643-1687. 2. Explorers.
3. Mississippi River—Discovery and exploration.] I. Title. II. Series.
F1030.5.J33J33 1994
977'.01'092—dc20   93-29699
[B]   CIP AC

CONTENTS

Never give in, never give in, never, never, never, never, never — in nothing great or small, large or petty — never give in....

— WINSTON CHURCHILL,
address at Harrow School, 1941

PREFACE

April 9, 1682. On that date, explorer René-Robert Cavelier, Sieur de La Salle, proudly implanted the flag of France and a wooden Christian cross at the mouth of the mighty Mississippi River, "the father of waters." It was his moment of triumph, the high point of his career.

With that simple ceremony, La Salle laid claim for France, in the name of King Louis XIV, to all of the vast territory whose rivers flowed into the Mississippi. The land he claimed, the fabulous Louisiana, was an area many times the size of his French homeland. For many years to come, it was to be the centerpiece for France's continuing dream of a great colonial empire in the New World.

La Salle, unlike the Spanish conquistadores Cortés and Pizarro and some of the early French and English explorers, was not a greedy seeker after gold. Glory, for its own sake, held little appeal for him. Nor was he especially interested in converting the Indians to Christianity. For La Salle, the appeal of exploring an untamed

King Louis XIV

continent lay in great enterprises: the search for a water route to China through the North American continent, the conquest of Mexico from Spain, and the triumph of France over all rival nations. For him, nothing less than a grand adventure would do, an adventure that would be a supreme test of his determination, his energy, his will.

To the poet Longfellow, La Salle's achievement could be summed up as "the life of a man of genius, resisting all temptations, laying aside all fears, heedless of all warnings, and pressing right on to accomplish his purpose."

La Salle becomes a more fascinating personality for us because his goals of conquest were boundless. His successes were enormous. He and his party were among the first Europeans to find their way into the interior of the continent. He explored the shores of the Great Lakes, may have been the first white man to see the Ohio River, and finally descended the Mississippi River to the Gulf of Mexico.

The story of La Salle is that of a man risking much in search of what he may have known was an impossible goal. Yet sternly, mercilessly, he pushed on, brushing aside all thought of harm to himself and to his men. The life he lived — unbending, single-minded, driven — is a fascinating chapter in the history of human adventure.

A view of Rouen, France, the birthplace of René-Robert Cavelier

12

CHAPTER ONE
THE
LURE
OF
CANADA

René-Robert Cavelier was born wealthy. He was the second son of a prosperous merchant in Rouen, France. From the time of his birth in November 1643, he had all the advantages that came with his family's favored social position. The title *Sieur de La Salle*, by which he is known to history, was taken from the name of the Caveliers' fashionable estate in the countryside.

As a boy, La Salle was a deeply religious Roman Catholic. Hoping to serve the Church as an overseas missionary, he joined the Society of Jesus (commonly known as the Jesuits). The Jesuits followed a difficult and demanding plan of education, one that sharpened La Salle's already quick mind, training him to write and to speak well.

But the Jesuits never were able to convince young La Salle to obey. Instead of following the wishes of the priests, he wanted to decide matters for himself and to command other people. Intelligent and proud, he became more and more restless. He came to dislike

The young René-Robert Cavelier,
Sieur de La Salle

 14

being a Jesuit. Finally, he did not even want to be a priest. When La Salle was twenty-two years old, his father died. No longer worried about hurting his father's feelings, La Salle left the Jesuit order.

According to French law at the time, a person joining a religious community gave up his right to inherit family wealth. So La Salle was forced to depend on his relatives for money, almost to live on an allowance from them. Proud and strong, he found it impossible to rely on other people, even those closest to him.

La Salle could have become a merchant in Rouen as his father had been. What really appealed to him, however, was travel and adventure. Because his older brother, Jean Cavelier, already was a priest in Canada, young Robert thought he might have a chance in the Americas to carve out an exciting and successful life of his own. In the spring of 1666, not yet twenty-three years old, La Salle sailed for Canada.

On his arrival there, the priests of his brother's religious community gave him a sizeable land grant on the St. Lawrence River, west of Montreal. In return, he agreed to recruit settlers from France to live on the land.

La Salle patiently began to clear the section of land he had set aside for his own use. As promised, he attracted new settlers. He engaged in profitable fur trading with the Indians. After only two years as a farmer and fur trader, he had become a wealthy man. If he had chosen to do so, he could have lived the rest of his life in ease and comfort. But La Salle was ambitious. He was still restless.

One day two Seneca Indians visiting his home told him of a great river, far away, that flowed into the sea. To the dreamer La Salle, the river might be the long-sought "passage to India" — an all-water route through the North American continent to the Pacific Ocean.

The Indians spoke to him of two rivers: the *Ohio,* or "Beautiful Water," and the *Missi-Sepe*, or "Big Water." Either or both, thought La Salle, might lead to the "Vermillion Sea," or Gulf of California. Beyond that was Asia: the Spice Islands and the fabled lands of China and India.

Although afire with enthusiasm, La Salle did not have enough money to organize such an ambitious expedition. Nor would the French governor living in Quebec help him. The Catholic priests of Montreal urged the passionate young adventurer to stay in Canada.

But La Salle had made up his mind. He sold all of his land holdings to an ironworker. With that money, he outfitted four canoes and hired fourteen men to accompany him on his voyage.

The governor asked La Salle to take on another party led by a Sulpician priest, François Dollier de

*Fur trading was an extremely
profitable enterprise for the
French in North America.*

Casson. The Sulpicians hoped to convert many Indians to Christianity. On July 6, 1669, the priests, with ten men and three canoes, gathered to depart with La Salle's group. Two more canoes, bearing Seneca Indian guides, traveled at the head of the column as the tiny band of French adventurers set out into the uncharted wilderness.

CHAPTER TWO
LA SALLE'S
FIRST WANDERINGS
IN THE
NEW WORLD

For most of the Frenchmen on the trip, exploring was a new experience. The food was strange: mostly boiled Indian corn seasoned with pieces of fish. To move between rivers and streams all the canoes and supplies had to be carried overland by hand. There was no shelter against the rain and cold winds. Still, they persisted.

One month after leaving Montreal, the explorers met a party of Seneca Indians. At the village of the Senecas, the Europeans were treated as honored guests. They feasted on dog meat and were given many gifts. As a special entertainment the Senecas brought in a captured warrior from a neighboring tribe. They bound him to a stake and for six hours slowly tortured him. Finally turning him loose, they caught him and stoned him to death. Then they ripped his body apart and ate him piece by piece.

Sickened by what they had seen and fearful of what might lie ahead for them, the Frenchmen left as soon as

La Salle met his fellow Frenchman Louis Jolliet at Niagra Falls. Jolliet told La Salle of his encounters with Indians along the shores of the Great Lakes.

20

they could. Their departure may, indeed, have been just what the Indians had in mind.

At an Indian village near Niagara Falls, they were surprised to meet two other Frenchmen. One was another former Jesuit priest, Louis Jolliet, who had become a fur trader and explorer. Jolliet told La Salle and the Sulpician priests about the Potawatomi Indians he had met along the shores of Lake Superior. They were, he said, uncivilized and in great need of becoming Christians.

Over the strong objections of La Salle, the Sulpicians decided to go northward to the upper Great Lakes to work with the people Jolliet had described. La Salle refused to go with them. Instead he chose to continue on toward his goal: the Ohio and Mississippi river valleys.

The parting of the two groups was friendly, marked by a Catholic mass led by one of the priests. The Sulpicians set off to the northwest, La Salle and his followers to the south.

One difficulty after another marked the journey of the Sulpicians. Finally, after a storm one night on Lake Erie, they landed exhausted on the beach, too tired even to move their baggage. By morning most of it, including the sacred objects for their altar, had been swept away into the lake.

Having failed to convert a single Indian, the missionaries returned to Montreal. Most of the city's population placed the blame for the Sulpicians' failure on La Salle, charging that he never should have deserted the priests.

Meanwhile, La Salle was also in trouble. Several of his men fled, frightened by stories told by the Senecas about dangers in the Ohio River valley. Some of the men found their way back to Montreal. Others took refuge from the snows and the cold winter among the Dutch and English settlers who had moved west across the Appalachian Mountains.

What La Salle did from 1669 through most of 1672 remains uncertain. Nor is it clear whether he was alone during those years. Based on lands he is said to have discovered, France laid claim to the entire Ohio valley. With little protest from Great Britain, the French then built Fort Duquesne (today's Pittsburgh) at the source of the Ohio River.

Although the exact path of La Salle's travels was not recorded, we do know that he lived entirely in the wilderness. He sailed on lakes that no white man had ever seen before. He hunted and fished. He slept out under the stars. He roasted dog meat over open fires. He lived with the Indians and learned their languages.

La Salle had been born to wealth. He had been educated out of ancient books about civilizations long dead. Now, surrounded by all the dangers of the North American wilderness, he finally believed that his life had real purpose.

*La Salle and his men making camp
in the wilderness of North America*

23

Records show that by December 1672, La Salle once again had returned to Montreal, but his deeds seem to have excited little comment among the city's inhabitants. He had not discovered a dramatic "passage to India." Moreover, some still blamed him for allowing the Sulpician priests to go off on their own, far from the protection of civilization.

La Salle's popularity probably had reached its lowest point, but better days lay ahead for him. In 1672, a new governor had been appointed for New France, the Count de Frontenac.

CHAPTER THREE
FRONTENAC
AND
LA SALLE

Like La Salle, the Count de Frontenac had major plans for the future. He hoped to build a fort on the shores of Lake Ontario to keep the Indians in check and to control the fur trade. The fort would make New France safer from Indian attacks. It could also make the few men who had complete control of the fur trade incredibly rich. As for Frontenac, he hoped to share in the greater glory of New France, as well as in the colony's wealth.

La Salle had plans of his own. In the course of his travels, he had become convinced that the Mississippi River emptied not into the Pacific Ocean but into the Gulf of Mexico. Therefore, a strong French fortress at the mouth of the Mississippi could be important. Almost certainly it could prevent foreign ships from entering or leaving the river without French permission. As a result, France would virtually control the heartland of the North American continent.

La Salle believed that if only he could achieve his

Count de Frontenac

26

goal, the entire trade of the region — the furs, the buffalo skins, the agricultural goods — would be in French hands. But even before that, La Salle reasoned, France must have a safe, secure stronghold in Canada. And that, he understood, was exactly the same view held by Frontenac. The two men knew they could help each other. They trusted and liked each other, each respecting the other's strengths. Soon they became close friends. They agreed to work together to gain control of the continent for France.

In July 1673, with La Salle's advice and help, Frontenac moved to put his plan into action. At a conference arranged by La Salle, Frontenac met with the chiefs of the Iroquois Indians.

The French governor arrived by water with the 120 canoes in his fleet carefully arranged in battle formation. With great pomp and dignity, Frontenac marched his entire force of 400 men, wearing their finest dress uniforms, in front of the awestruck Indians. There were parades, military music, and lavish gifts for the Indian men, women, and children.

The leaders of the five Iroquois nations — Mohawks, Oneidas, Onondagas, Cayugas, and Senecas — all saw Frontenac as a man of peace, but one whose friendship was backed by military might. They agreed to let him build a fortress at Cataraqui (today's Kingston, Ontario).

Soon the fort was built, commanding Lake Ontario and seriously limiting contacts between the English and

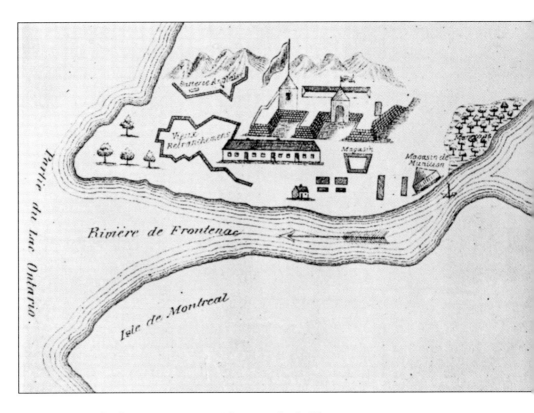

The fortress Cataraqui (near today's Kingston, Ontario) was renamed Fort Frontenac in honor of Count de Frontenac.

the Indians. As a result, the fur trade fell quickly into the hands of the French.

In reward for La Salle's help, Frontenac sent his friend to Paris to meet with King Louis XIV and Colbert, France's minister of finance. During the visit La Salle was formally admitted to membership in the French nobility. He was also given the authority to govern Cataraqui, or as he gratefully renamed the new outpost, Fort Frontenac. Finally, he was given exclusive trading rights over all the nearby lands.

Overnight the grant made La Salle one of the most powerful men in Canada. The location of the territory he was to rule gave him almost complete control of the fur trade with the Indians. If he had been content with the privileges of a merchant and "lord of the manor," his fortune would have been ensured for life. La Salle, however, had even grander dreams.

*The area around Fort Frontenac
was developed into farmland
and a fur trading center.*

CHAPTER FOUR

BLOOD, TOIL, TEARS, AND SWEAT

For three years, beginning in 1675, La Salle worked to develop Fort Frontenac. He brought the Iroquois Indians and French families to settle close to the fortress. He arranged for the clearing and planting of farmland. To expand the fur trade, he had four ships built to sail Lake Ontario. Nearly 200 miles (322 km) from Montreal, he reigned without supervision as lord of his own little empire.

In 1677, La Salle returned to France. He asked for the right to explore lands along the Mississippi River and even farther, perhaps all the way to Mexico. King Louis XIV gave him permission to explore and also to build as many fortresses as necessary. The king warned La Salle, however, not to start too many new colonies, something he feared might spread the French colonial empire in North America too thinly.

In 1678, with Count Frontenac's help, La Salle began gathering men and supplies for his expedition. He sent Father Louis Hennepin, an adventurous

The Griffon *was finally built, loaded,
and ready to sail in August 1679.*

Franciscan priest, to begin building a fort at Niagara Falls. When La Salle finally arrived, he ordered the construction of a powerful 45-ton ship, the *Griffon*. With five large cannons, it was to be a "floating fortress," a ship that would carry furs but also frighten the Indians, making them unwilling to risk warfare with the French. Henry de Tonty, an Italian military man who admired La Salle, was put in charge of constructing the *Griffon*. He also became La Salle's second-in-command.

At last, in August 1679, the ship was ready. La Salle and his men sailed into Lake Erie. They made their way to Fort Michilimackinac and from there to Green Bay. Soon they had filled the ship's hold with precious furs, ready for sale.

On September 18, 1679, La Salle sent the *Griffon*, manned by several soldiers, back to Fort Frontenac. They were to use the profits from the valuable cargo to pay whatever debts he owed and then return to their starting point, Green Bay. The guns of the *Griffon* thundered a farewell salvo and, with storm clouds gathering on the horizon, the ship sailed away.

Possibly lost in a storm, the *Griffon* never was seen again. To this day its fate remains a mystery.

* * *

After the *Griffon* had set sail, La Salle, with fourteen men and four canoes, continued southward to explore

AN
ACCOUNT
OF
Monſieur *de la* SALLE's
LAST
Expedition and DISCOVERIES
IN
North AMERICA.
Preſented to the *French* King,

And Publiſhed by the

Chevalier *Tonti*, Governour of Fort St. Lo-
uis, in the Province of the *Iſlinois*.

Made *Engliſh* from the *Paris* Original.

ALSO
The ADVENTURES of the Sieur *de*
MONTAUBAN, Captain of the *French*
Buccaneers on the Coaſt of *Guinea*, in the
Year 1695.

LONDON,
Printed for *J. Tonſon* at the *Judge's Head*, and *S. Buckly*,
at the *Dolphin* in *Fleet-ſtreet*, and *R. Knaplock*, at the
Angel and *Crown* in St. *Paul's Church-Yard*. 1698.

The title page from Henri de Tonti's book
An Account of Monsieur de La Salle's Last
Expedition and Discoveries in North America

34

the shoreline of Lake Michigan. A force under Tonty, meanwhile, was sent separately to collect more furs.

For a time, nothing went well for La Salle's group. First they were driven into rocks by fierce winds, then threatened by hostile Indians. Without food, they were reduced to frightening buzzards away so they could eat the mangled remains of a deer killed by wolves.

Tonty later rejoined the group, reporting that the *Griffon* never had reached Michilimackinac. Shortly after hearing that news, La Salle became separated from the expedition while hunting for an Indian trail. It was only by good fortune that he stumbled upon his companions once again. Another time a fire that had been lighted to warm the wigwam he shared with Father Hennepin ignited the reed mats on which the two men were sleeping. Fortunately, they both escaped. Finally, a member of La Salle's own force tried to kill him but failed.

Even more serious events were to follow. To build a ship to sail down the Mississippi, La Salle desperately needed anchors and rigging. Without them, he thought, his whole expedition might fail. As a result, in March 1680, he set out on foot for Fort Frontenac, a distance of 1,000 miles (1,600 km).

The journey, as La Salle described it, was agonizing. He and his men marched by day and slept on the open ground at night. They pushed through bramble thickets and climbed rocks covered with ice and snow.

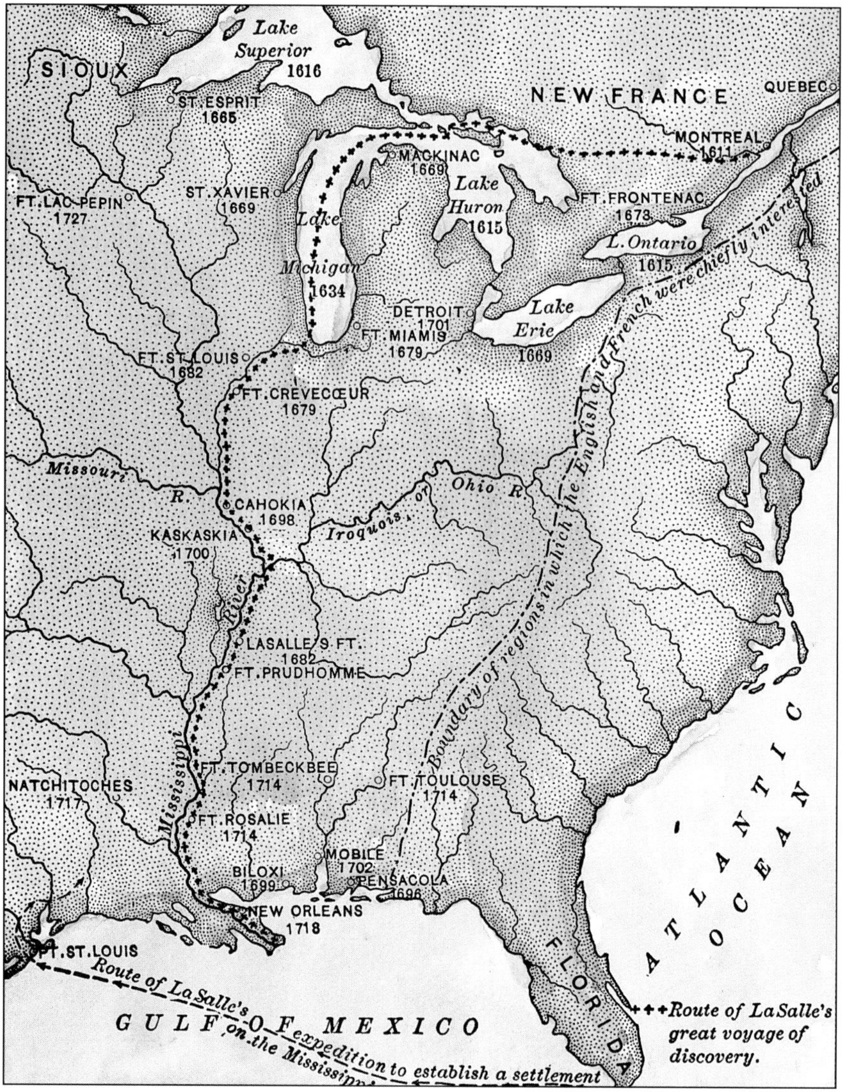
Lake Superior 1616
SIOUX
ST. ESPRIT 1665
NEW FRANCE
QUEBEC
MONTREAL 1611
MACKINAC 1669
Lake Huron 1615
FT. FRONTENAC 1673
L. Ontario 1615
ST. XAVIER 1669
FT. LAC PEPIN 1727
Lake Michigan 1634
DETROIT 1701
FT. MIAMIS 1679
Lake Erie 1669
FT. ST. LOUIS 1682
FT. CREVECŒUR 1679
Missouri R.
CAHOKIA 1698
KASKASKIA 1700
Iroquois, or Ohio R.
Mississippi River
LASALLE'S FT. 1682
FT. PRUDHOMME
Boundary of regions in which the English and French were chiefly interested
FT. TOMBECKBEE 1714
FT. TOULOUSE 1714
NATCHITOCHES 1717
FT. ROSALIE 1714
MOBILE 1702
BILOXI 1699
PENSACOLA 1696
NEW ORLEANS 1718
FT. ST. LOUIS
Route of La Salle's expedition to establish a settlement on the Mississippi
GULF OF MEXICO
FLORIDA
ATLANTIC OCEAN
Route of La Salle's great voyage of discovery.

This map traces La Salle's voyage of discovery down the Mississippi River.

Sometimes for whole days they waded through marshland, the water waist-deep or even higher. As the weather grew warmer, rain fell down on them in sheets. Of the soldiers in his party, only La Salle and one other man did not become desperately ill.

Finally, after a journey of sixty-five days across one third of the continent, he and his tiny party emerged from the wilderness at Fort Frontenac. The news that greeted La Salle was shocking. His creditors, thinking him dead, had seized all of his property. Even his own lawyers had cheated him. Some people considered him insane.

Refusing to accept defeat, La Salle made his way to Montreal. In less than a week, he had borrowed enough money to buy the shipbuilding supplies he needed.

In August 1680, La Salle began the 1,000-mile (1,600-km) journey back to the west. He brought with him a party of twenty-five men, including carpenters, masons, and soldiers. He also brought all the materials needed for constructing a sailing ship to descend the mighty Mississippi River.

*Father Louis Hennepin ventured along
the upper Mississippi River to
collect furs and to explore.*

CHAPTER FIVE
THE
ROAD
TO
GLORY

Arriving at last in the country of the Illinois Indians, La Salle expected to be greeted warmly by Tonty and his crew. Instead, at one Indian village after another, he found scenes of horror. The Iroquois nations had struck in a ruthless series of raids. With the Illinois warriors away, the Iroquois had tortured and killed women and children. They had destroyed the cornfields and burned the huts. Wolves now roamed freely among the corpses. Buzzards feasted.

And where was Tonty? Where was Father Hennepin, who, at La Salle's command, had gone to collect furs and to explore the shores of the upper Mississippi? La Salle searched in vain for his comrades. Then, with cold weather coming on, he set up a temporary headquarters near Lake Michigan, where he spent the winter of 1680–81.

In early March, La Salle set out again to find the other Frenchmen. Traveling in the open prairie, with the brilliant sun reflecting off the snow, he and several

*On February 13, 1682,
La Salle launched a tiny
fleet onto the Mississippi.*

of his men became snow-blind. It took many days before
they recovered.

During La Salle's illness, Indian warriors who had
befriended him brought good news. Although the
French base had been destroyed, Tonty had been seen
alive. As soon as La Salle was well enough to travel, he
set out for Michilimackinac. There, to his delight, he
found his loyal Italian companion in perfect health and

overjoyed at their reunion. Father Hennepin, however, had left for France to claim credit for his own explorations and, as it turned out, also for some La Salle had made.

Returning to Montreal, La Salle and Tonty pleaded for more money, supplies, and men to achieve their vital goal: a voyage down the Mississippi. With the support of Count Frontenac, they borrowed enough money for supplies. They also hired a force of twenty-two Frenchmen and thirty Indians.

By then La Salle had given up his plan of constructing a large ship for his voyage. Instead, he placed himself at the head of a formation of frail but fast-moving canoes. On February 13, 1682, he launched his tiny fleet into the powerful current of the Mississippi. The caravan was carried along swiftly past the mouth of the Missouri River. Farther downstream the rolling tide of the river was swelled by the broad, slow-moving waters of the Ohio River.

At first the party of explorers stopped only to hunt the wild turkeys, swans, deer, and buffalo so plentiful along the riverbanks. Then they began to meet with various Indian tribes. One tribe, the Arkansas, feasted and entertained them for three days.

About 100 miles (160 km) beyond the mouth of the Arkansas River, they came across another group, the Taensas. Those Indians worshiped the sun, and their chief considered himself a living descendant of the sun god. La Salle and his men gave the chief generous gifts and were treated well by the Taensas.

The fleet of canoes traveled swiftly southward along the river. At each new Indian village, La Salle planted a large cross and raised the flag of King Louis XIV. Each time, a priest led the singing of the hymns, and three salvos of shots were fired from the explorers' muskets. Always, La Salle claimed the new territories in the name of the king of France, formally taking ownership of the new lands for his nation. The Indians whose lands he was claiming could only stand by, not understanding the meaning of the strange ceremony that would eventually take away from them their ancient homelands.

On April 6, 1682, the French explorers came upon the delta of the Mississippi River, the present site of New Orleans. There the river divided into three channels, all marked by the smell of seawater. La Salle knew that he was close to his goal. On April 9, he reached the Gulf of Mexico.

With great rejoicing among the Frenchmen, he planted a cross. At its base, he buried deep in the ground a copper plate engraved with the coat of arms of France. Then, in a simple speech, he took possession of the entire valley of the Mississippi River which, in honor of King Louis XIV, he called Louisiana. After the speech, there were solemn hymns led by the priests. Finally, the soldiers exploded with shouts of *"Vive le roi!"* ("Long live the King!") They fired salvos of shots

La Salle claims the Mississippi for France and King Louis XIV, naming the area Louisiana in the his honor.

into the air and cheered the triumph of their great leader, La Salle.

On that spring day along the Mississippi in 1682, René-Robert Cavelier, Sieur de La Salle, laid claim to an incredible domain. It extended from the Allegheny Mountains on the east to the Rocky Mountains on the west, and from the Great Lakes on the north to the Rio Grande and the Gulf of Mexico on the south. One day the area would provide boundless wealth in farmland and mineral resources. With a few words, spoken in a simple ceremony before a cluster of puzzled Indians and a handful of his own countrymen, La Salle had given France title to a mighty empire. He had also entered his name forever in the history of discovery and exploration.

CHAPTER SIX

FINAL
VOYAGES

It was one thing to lay claim to an empire, quite another thing to govern it. La Salle was determined to see his dream of empire come true, but there were enormous obstacles still in the way.

The return voyage up the Mississippi proved to be a nightmare. At first there was little food but alligator meat. Angry Indians followed at the Frenchmen's heels, sometimes firing arrows at them. La Salle, despite his strong body and iron will, fell desperately ill. For forty days, he hovered on the brink of death, but he would not give in. For months afterward, he remained badly weakened.

Making his way northward, he was far too ill to think about a trip to France. Yet only by reporting his discoveries to the king could he possibly win financial support to build a city at the mouth of the Mississippi.

Meanwhile, the political situation in Quebec had changed dramatically. Enemies of La Salle and Count

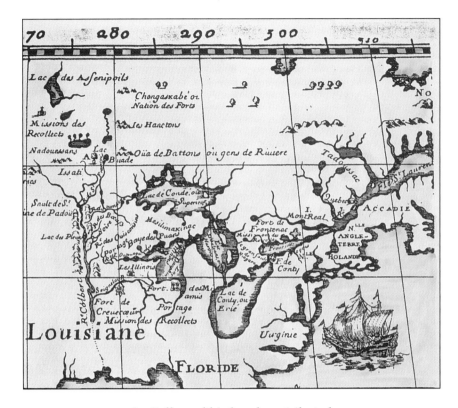

La Salle and his band contributed
greatly to the expansion of French
territory in North America.

Frontenac had convinced authorities in France to replace Frontenac as governor. His successor was LeFebvre de la Barre, a greedy, jealous old man who hoped to block La Salle's plans and to seize his property.

Acting swiftly, La Barre seized Fort Frontenac. Then

he refused to send the ammunition and supplies La Salle had been requesting. Instead, he suggested to the Iroquois that they seek out the explorer and kill him.

In the early autumn of 1683, La Salle finally managed to reach Quebec. Departing swiftly from the city, he managed to elude La Barre and set sail for France to plead his cause.

At the court of Louis XIV, the dignified, impressive La Salle was received as a hero. His deeds in the wilderness of North America became the talk of Paris. He wrote about his adventures and gave lengthy interviews.

King Louis hoped to challenge his nation's strongest enemies, the Spaniards, in their powerful Mexican colony. He also hoped to build a French stronghold on the lower Mississippi. To achieve these goals, he granted La Salle a fleet of four ships, including the *Joly*, a vessel of thirty-six guns with a crew of seventy.

Also included in the force were soldiers, civilian volunteers, and even women and children to help establish a French colony in Louisiana. Several missionaries agreed to travel with the expedition, including La Salle's own brother, the Abbé Jean Cavelier.

On July 24, 1684, the expedition set sail for North America. By November, the fleet entered the Gulf of Mexico, a sea declared forbidden to all Europeans but Spaniards by King Philip II of Spain.

*La Salle was received as a hero at the
court of Louis XIV after reporting
his successes to the French king.*

Once inside the gulf, a serious problem developed for the French fleet. When La Salle first canoed down to the mouth of the Mississippi from Canada, he had been unable to map the river's exact location. The pilots of his ships were not familiar with the region, either. As a result, the French vessels sailed past the river's entrance, landing far to the west, probably near the site of today's Corpus Christi, Texas.

Shortly afterward, La Salle's main supply ship ran aground on a sandbar and was destroyed. It was a serious blow, leaving the party without vital tools and weapons. La Salle, admitting that he was lost, decided to build a rough fortress and at least start to form a colony.

As month followed month, the unhappy company's misfortunes grew more serious: food and water were unsanitary. Disease spread rapidly. Every day four or five people died. The Indians howled through the night, stole blankets and other items, and set fires around the camp. Attempts to raise food by farming generally failed. Deadly rattlesnakes terrorized the settlers. To make matters worse, the *Joly*, sent to look for supplies, embarked instead for France. Not long afterward, La Salle's fourth and last ship was wrecked and its entire crew lost.

Without ships there was only one way the settlers could ever hope to return safely to their homeland.

La Salle leaving a Texas fort in 1687

They had to find the Mississippi River and then make
their way northward to Canada.

In January 1687, La Salle and the remainder of his
once proud expedition set out looking for help. They left

behind them about twenty settlers, many too weak for such travel, including all the surviving women and children. The scene of their farewell was one of deep sadness. Those who left and those who stayed behind knew they might never again see each other.

For more than two months, La Salle and his men marched northeastward toward the Mississippi. Then, one day in the middle of March, there was a fatal quarrel over food involving Moranget, La Salle's hot-tempered nephew. That night three men waited until Moranget was asleep. Then they killed him with an ax. Having done the bloody deed, they realized there would be no way to hide from La Salle the murder of his own nephew. The great French commander surely would not allow the killers to return unpunished to civilization. Therefore, they decided that he, too, would have to die.

The next day, March 18, 1687, La Salle went to look for his nephew. One of the murderers distracted him by shouting insults. Then the other two, hiding in ambush behind high reeds, fired their pistols. Shot through the head, René-Robert Cavelier, Sieur de La Salle, died instantly. He was forty-three years old.

The assassins stripped his body of clothing and valuables and then left it unburied for the wolves and buzzards to devour.

One of the killers fled to live with the Indians. The other two were shot to death by a member of the expe-

*La Salle was shot to death by two men
in his expedition who ambushed him.*

52

dition. Eventually the survivors, including La Salle's brother, the Abbé Cavelier, managed to make their way to Quebec. From there they returned home to France.

In late April 1689, a party of Spanish soldiers discovered the remains of the makeshift French fort in Texas. It was a scene of death and destruction. Later the Spaniards learned from French deserters living among the Indians that two months earlier the camp had been destroyed. Almost all of the settlers had perished from disease or at the hands of Indians who carried out a bloody raid there. Even today the fate of a few French children, known to have been rescued by Indian women, remains a mystery.

La Salle

AFTERMATH

So ended La Salle's dream of founding a great French empire in the heartland of America. He had established forts, organized Indian alliances, traveled where no other white man ever had been before. Yet of all those efforts, little survived. Others had to do the often dull, painstaking work of planting crops and building cities, tasks for which the French commander had neither the time nor the patience. All that remained of his years of heroism was the example of his energy and of his unconquerable will.

La Salle had concentrated his entire being toward the achievement of a single ambitious goal. With patience and courage, he had braved hunger, fatigue, disease, cold, heat, and the jealous plotting of his enemies. No hardship was too great, no suffering too severe as, joylessly he sacrificed everything else to achieve his ends.

A complicated man, La Salle had no wife. He trusted nobody but himself. He listened to no advice and cared not at all for pleasure or for popularity. Driven to succeed regardless of the risk to his own safety or that of his men, he aroused either intense loyalty or great hatred. In that sense, like other deeply committed dreamers and adventurers of history, he carried within his personality the seeds of his greatest triumphs, and also of his own destruction.

IMPORTANT DATES

1643	René-Robert Cavelier, Sieur de La Salle is born in Rouen, France.
1666	La Salle sails for Canada.
1669	Sets out into uncharted Canadian wilderness with a party of Sulpician priests.
1669–73	Wanderings in area of Ohio River.
1673	La Salle and Frontenac establish a fortress at the site of present Kingston, Ontario.
1675–77	La Salle organizes Fort Frontenac.
1677	La Salle returns to France. Louis XIV gives him the authority to lead an expedition to find an outlet to the sea at the mouth of the Mississippi River.
1679	The *Griffon* is sent to Fort Frontenac, but never arrives.
1680	La Salle survives the fearful journey from Fort Frontenac to Montreal and returns, bringing soldiers and supplies.
1682–February 13	Launches fleet southward into Mississippi River.
1682–April 9	La Salle implants the flag of France at the mouth of the Mississippi River.
1683	La Salle is received as a hero in Paris at court of Louis XIV.
1684–July 24	Sets sail for the New World, hoping to establish a French stronghold on the lower Mississippi and to challenge Spanish authority in Mexico.
1687–January	Following months of Indian raids and disease on the Texas coast of the Gulf of Mexico, sets out in search of route to Canada.
1687–March 18	La Salle is assassinated by members of his own expedition.

FOR FURTHER READING

FOR OLDER READERS

Brebner, John. *The Explorers of North America, 1492–1806*. New York: Macmillan, 1933.

Childs, Marquis W. *Mighty Mississippi: Biography of a River*. New Haven: Ticknor & Fields, 1982.

Cox, Isaac J. *The Journeys of René-Robert Cavelier, Sieur de La Salle*. 2 vols. New York: A. S. Barnes, 1905.

Lomask, Milton. *Great Lives: Exploration*. New York: Charles Scribner's Sons, 1988.

Munro, William Bennett. *Crusaders of New France*. New Haven: Yale University Press, 1921.

Parkman, Francis. *La Salle and the Discovery of the Great West*. Vol. 3 of *France and England in North America* (7 vols.). New York: Frederick Ungar, 1965.

FOR MIDDLE READERS

Coulter, Tony. *La Salle and the Explorers of the Mississippi*. New York: Chelsea House, 1991.

Nolan, Jeannette. *La Salle and the Grand Enterprise*. North Bellmore, N.Y.: Marshall Cavendish, 1991.

INDEX

ABOUT
THE
AUTHOR

William Jay Jacobs has studied history at Harvard, Yale, and Princeton and holds a doctorate from Columbia. He has held fellowships with the Ford Foundation and the National Endowment for the Humanities and served as a Fulbright Fellow in India. In addition to broad teaching experience in public and private secondary schools, he has taught at Rutgers University, at Hunter College, and at Harvard. Dr. Jacobs presently is Visiting Fellow in the Department of History at Yale.

Among his previous books for young readers are biographies of such diverse personalities as Abraham Lincoln, Eleanor Roosevelt, Edgar Allan Poe, Hannibal, Hitler, and Mother Teresa. His *America's Story* and *History of the United States* are among the nation's most widely used textbooks.

In the Franklin Watts First Book series, he is the author of *Magellan, Cortés, Pizarro, La Salle, Champlain,* and *Coronado.*